The Illustrated Dictionary of LOBSTERING

The Illustrated Dictionary of LOBSTERING

Kendall Merriam

Photographs by Ed Wheaton

International Standard Book Number: 0-87027-192-X
Library of Congress Catalog Card Number: 78-61525

The Cumberland Press, Inc. d/b/a
Bond Wheelwright Company
136 Main Street
Freeport, Maine 04032

second printing 1982

Text and Cover designed by Bonnie Spiegel
Line Drawings by William Morris
DEDICATION PAGE PHOTO: EDWARD W. COFFIN, OWLS HEAD, ME.

PRINTED IN THE UNITED STATES OF AMERICA

Frontispiece: Lobster Boat

Respectfully dedicated to

Woodbury Snow

of Rockland, Maine & Metinic Island

He caught codfish while I caught dogfish.

ACKNOWLEDGMENTS

The first credit for this book goes to a place, not to people. I have been going to Metinic Island off and on since I was eight years of age. It is a place of surpassing beauty and interest—eight miles off Spruce Head, Maine. There I learned most of what I know about the lobstering industry.

I want to thank the people associated with Metinic who have given me information, fun and sustenance: Ralph and Loella Post, Woodbury and Judy Post, Frank and Bonnie Post, and Ralph and Mary Post.

Other people who gave many definitions, terms and information about earlier lobstering are Edward Coffin of Owl's Head, Francis "Joe" Nash of Owl's Head, David Littleton-Taylor of Lincolnville Beach, Marshall Merriam of Owl's Head, Frank Milan of Deer Isle, and John Wheaton of Swan's Island.

Stephen Cook, and Bill and Chris Butman provided special recipes.

Al Landry of Richmond, and Phyllis Merriam

provided criticism and support. My editors, Bill and Mary Lou Morris, charted waters far from Texas to bring this book to fruition. My parents, Paul and Doris Merriam, provided crucial logistical support when I was writing the first edition.

I want to especially thank Ed Wheaton, the book's photographer, for pushing me along when I got bogged down. He saw from the very beginning that it would be a worthwhile book.

Finally to Woodbury Snow, "The King of Metinic," who took me fishing off the South End once. On one side of the boat he caught seven codfish, while on the other I caught seven dogfish.

INTRODUCTION

One day, some summer soon, a lobsterman will come back halfway through hauling, frustrated and enraged. He will say, "There was no sense hauling, I only got two lobsters in fifty traps."

That is a far cry from the summer of 1952, when my brother, Paul, hauled a trap in the cove at Metinic which had eighty-two lobsters in it, fourteen of them counters.

And that is a long way from when men picked them up from under the seaweed, gaffed them in the shallows, and caught a dozen in fifteen minutes on hoop nets. Lobsters used to wash ashore in windrows after the big storms—but that hasn't happened in many decades. I have once seen Frank Post pick a lobster from the seaweed on a low dreen tide, but I am undoubtedly fortunate to have seen that.

The appetite for lobster is increasing as the supply is decreasing. In a big restaurant in Miami one can cost $25.00, while in Maine it can sell for $1.89 a pound. The invention of the lobster tank put the beast all over the eastern half of the country, in restaurants and stores. This steady increase in demand has been met as best it can be by the fishermen who put out more and more traps, build better boats to fish in harder weather, and hire help to make the work go more efficiently.

All this, of course, has put an incredible strain on the lobster supply. Some men have teams fishing 3,000 traps. Some areas are almost completely fished out. Though there is disagreement at what age a lobster breeds, it seems fairly clear that the lobsters of seven years, or when they may first be caught, have probably bred only once if at all. This is confirmed by a statement of one lobsterman that they are catching ninety-five per cent of the legal lobsters in any given year. The lobsters are being fished out, possibly to extinction, unless some measures are taken by the lobsterman himself such as trap limits, closed seasons, increase in the legal size. What may well happen, is described by a question put to me by my wife, Phyllis, one evening when we were discussing the book and the lobstering industry in general. She said, "Do you think any of the children of the lobstermen we know will be able to fish?"

This is an important question for it has been the carrying-on from generation to generation of the skills of lobstering which have allowed us to enjoy the feast. If the breeding stock is fished out or destroyed and the fishermen have to go on to other occupations, will the skills survive the long period of waiting for the commercially viable numbers to return? That is a question only the future can answer.

This book is in every sense of the word a tribute to the men and women of the lobstering industry. It is also a book for tourists who might want to know more about the delicious creature they devour so readily when in Maine. It in no sense pretends to be complete, though the list of terms was checked by people ranging in age from their twenties to their eighties. There are terms we have missed, and some which are localisms, and we have included some words which are not general to the coast.

When I was in the seventh or eighth grade, I wrote a little school paper called "Lobstering on Metinic." My Mother found this and saved it and showed it to me in 1973, when I was writing my *Brief Dictionary of Lobstering,* a twelve-page mimeographed pamphlet that is the direct predecessor to this book. That earliest paper is a brief description of the lobstering process and the equipment used. It is also a predecessor, though consciously forgotten, to this book. I hope you like it.

Kendall A. Merriam

The Illustrated Dictionary of LOBSTERING

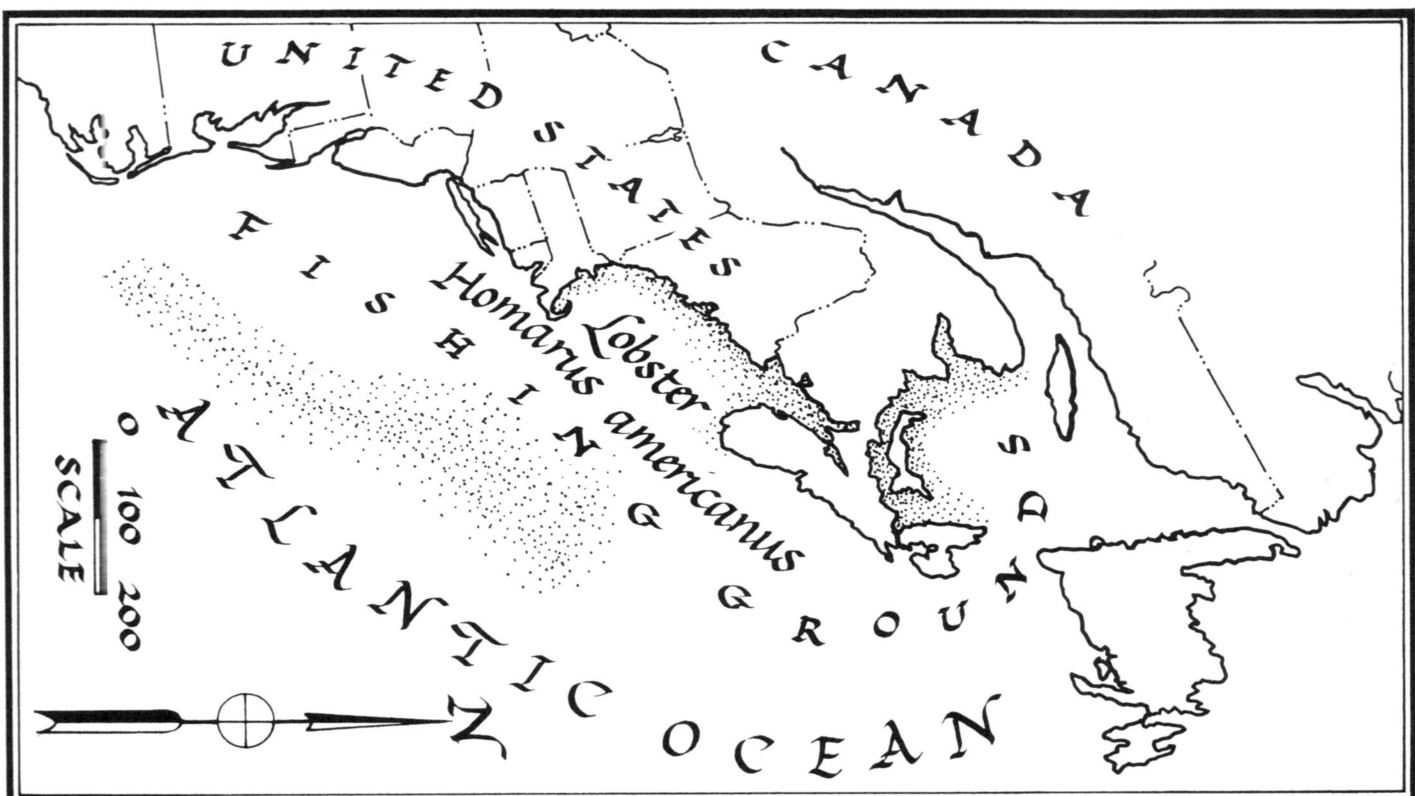
UNITED STATES
CANADA
FISHING GROUNDS
Lobster
Homarus americanus
ATLANTIC OCEAN
0 100 200
SCALE

A

A-Frame An A-shaped steel frame attached to the stern of the lobster boat to run out the gear for shrimping and scalloping. Also on a dragger for groundfish.

Airing Up Wind breezing up, not necessarily the beginning of a storm.

Alewife *(Pomolobus pseudoharengus).* A river herring that used to run up almost all of the streams in the Gulf of Maine; now only in a few, most notably at Warren and Damariscotta Mills and Orland. Alewives are sold to the lobstermen by the bushel for bait, and many fishermen say they fish better than brim or salt herring. Also used as bait on halibut trawls. Some are smoked and sold for human consumption.

Anchor A heavy weight used to hold a boat securely in place. Lobster fishermen carry a small anchor to hold fast to bottom in case of emergency.

Anchor Rode A piece of line used for anchoring.

Apron A covering the fisherman uses, from the chest to the knees, to keep water and gurry off his clothing. Usually made of rubber or plastic; formerly made of oilskin and called a barvel.

Arm A device for building round traps on. It consists of heavy timber fastened to the wall in the shop; or secured in a free-standing frame. The frames of the trap are placed on the board and the laths are nailed to the frame. It is not necessary to use an arm to build a square trap.

Ash Point Piazza A derogatory name given to the early glass and wooden houses (cabins) on lobster boats in an era when most boats had sprayhoods. The Ash Point referred to in this definition is in Owls Head, Maine, and according to lobstermen from other parts of the coast, this term is a localism.

B

Bait Fish used as a lure in lobster traps or on a trawl.

Bait Bag A small, knit, mesh bag that is filled with bait and placed on the bait string of the trap by means of the bait iron. The bait is often herring. Also called bait pocket. See photograph.

Bait Barrel A barrel or half-barrel used either in the bait house or on board the boat to carry bait. A box may be used instead of a barrel. See photograph.

Bait Box A box which stands on legs and holds the bait and is usually on board the boat. It makes a convenient platform for filling the bait bags or putting bait directly on the string. Also may refer to stackable plastic boxes that are used to carry bait on

Bait Bag

Bait Box

board the boat. These plastic boxes are replacing the bait barrel because they are easier and cleaner to handle. Bait box also refers to a small box made of laths, which is filled with bait and placed in the trap. Serves the same function as the bait bag, although not as commonly used. See photograph.

Bait Hook Another term for bait iron.

Bait House A building which has bins, boxes, or barrels filled with bait. Most lobstermen get their bait

Bait Barrel

from a dealer who keeps a bait house by his wharf. Some lobstermen have their own bait houses.

Bait Iron A device for threading the bait bag, or whole bait, onto the bait string. It consists of a handle, often a piece of an old oar, and a long metal spike which has a hole near the end. The fisherman sticks the iron through the bait bag, then threads the bait string through the hole in the iron, and pulls the bait string through the bag. Also called bait hook, bait needle, bait spear. See photograph.

Bait Iron

Bait Juice A brine that gathers in the bait barrel or box caused by the fish decomposing and mixing with the salt that is used as a preservative. Some bait boxes have plugs to drain out the bait juice. It is an irritant to any cuts on the lobsterman's hands. Also called "the pickle."

Bait Line Another term for bait string.

Bait Needle Another term for bait iron.

Bait Pocket Another term for bait bag.

Bait Spear Another term for bait iron.

Bait String A piece of twine attached to the bottom of the trap on which the bait bag is strung. The end of the string is then wound around the button or the cleat.

Bait Tub A container that serves the same function as the bait barrel or bait box.

Baiting-Up A term used to describe filling the bait bags, sometimes done the night before hauling, and sometimes in the morning.

Baked Stuffed Lobster One of the more common ways of cooking a lobster, especially in restaurants. The belly and underside of the tail are split open while the lobster is alive and are filled with a stuffing and baked. See cooking section.

Ballast Cement that has been poured into the bottom of wooden traps to make them sink. Formerly flat rocks were used, and still are occasionally. Wire traps, having no buoyancy, only need a couple of bricks to keep them down and flat on the bottom. See photograph.

Balling-the-Bait A descriptive term for the way a bait bag looks when it is being filled. Sometimes fishermen hire others to bait up for them. Payment is made per bag. Also called baiting-up.

Band Rubber band used in place of a plug to secure lobster claws. Also called elastic. See photograph.

Bander A tool, not unlike pliers, used for applying bands to the lobster claw.

Barnacle A small, white, shelled crustacean which clings to the bottom of lobster boats. The barnacle fouls and slows the boats; also clings to buoys, toggles, traps; as well as lobsters' shells.

Barvel The old name for apron. It was usually made from oilskin and kept the front of the lobsterman's clothes dry while he was hauling.

Bedroom Trap Another term for parlor trap.

Bell A small bell, which was often kept on board to warn others approaching in the fog. Compressed air horns are more frequently used today.

Bell Buoy A large navigational buoy placed in the water by the Coast Guard to warn of rocks, or to enable the fisherman to tell where he is. Also used to mark a channel. Often the lobsterman will "make for the buoy" in the fog, rain, or snow.

Berried Lobster A female lobster with eggs on her

Ballast

Band

tail. The eggs resemble small berries. These egg-bearing females must be thrown back overboard. Occasionally a lobsterman has been known to wash off the eggs and sell the lobster, but more enlightened lobstermen realize the value of the young for the economic survival of the industry.

Big Tides Higher than normal tides which make the current underrun the buoys.

Bilge The area below the platform down to the inside of the hull.

Bilge Pump Either a hand pump, or a battery-operated automatic pump with a float switch, used to remove water in the bilge. See photograph.

Binding-On The process of tying the warp onto the bridle.

Bilge Pump

Bitt A post with two arms which is used on the boat or dock to tie a line to.

Blind Head A head across the end of the trap with no opening which is used in place of laths. See photograph.

Block A marine term for pulley. See block and tackle, and hydraulic power block.

Block and Tackle A system of ropes and pulleys (blocks) used to increase the hauling power over a

Blind Head

small distance. Frequently used to haul boats up on a marine railway or to lift bait and other heavy objects.

Blowing A word used frequently by the lobsterman to talk about the wind. He might say, "It's blowing a mite," when it is a moderate wind. If the weather is really foul and no one is out, he might say, "It's blowin' a gale." Sometimes it's heard, "It's blowy out there today."

Blue Lobster A lobster which is blue in color, one of the rarities of the sea. Though no one knows the exact percentage some say, conveniently, one-in-a-million. Lobsters also occasionally have yellow, green, red, or white shells. Lobsters having two-colors, split down the middle lengthwise, have also been seen.

Boaht A common Maine pronunciation of the word boat, now dying out.

Body The forward shell of the lobster containing the brain, heart, and stomach. This is properly known as the carapace.

Boiled Lobster The simplest and most common way of cooking lobster. See cooking section.

Bottom A term that refers to the floor of the sea on which the traps are set. The bottom is described as a rocky, sandy, or mud bottom. Also refers to the underside of the hull.

Bottom Paint A copper paint applied to the bottom of wooden lobster boats to prevent fouling by barnacles and other marine organisms. Also helps prevent marine borers or torpedo worms. Usually applied once a year. Also called copper paint.

Bow Curved pieces of wood fastened to the frame of a lobster trap at the base. The laths are nailed to the bows to make a half-round trap. Formerly the bows were made of alder or spruce boughs; now are made of steamed-oak. See photograph of head.

Branding Iron An iron which after being heated in the fire, or electrically, is used to brand the lobsterman's license number into the trap and the buoy. See photograph.

Breakers Waves coming ashore on ledges or the

Branding Iron

mainland. The sound of breakers are used by lobstermen to tell where the ledges are in fog.

Breeze-Up The term breeze-up is used when the lobsterman is out hauling and the wind rises, making the fishing difficult.

Bridle Line or chain going over the boat's bow for attaching the painter. Also the line tied to each side of the end bow on the trap to which the warp is tied in order to haul the trap up evenly. See photograph.

Brim Lobster bait. The head, backbone, and tail of the redfish (*Sebastes marinus*) from which the fillets have been taken. It is used as bait most of the year when herring and alewives are not available.

Bulkhead A marine term for the wall between the cockpit and the cuddy. Also any wall on the boat.

JOE

Buoy A float, usually made of styrofoam or cedar wood, to hold up the end of the warp for hauling and identification.

Buoy Colors The specific combination of buoy colors registered with the state by each lobsterman, so he can tell his traps from those belonging to others. The buoy colors also must be displayed in a prominent position on the lobster boat. See colors.

Butt Block The block of wood that joins the planks on the inside of the hull. These blocks are always staggered to maintain strength.

Button A short piece of lath nailed with one nail to the trap to allow it to turn and serve as a trap door latch.

C

Cage A framework of bronze rods surrounding the lobster boat's propeller to prevent the propeller from cutting off or fouling on warp. See photograph.

Can Buoy A navigational buoy used to mark channels. Round, black cylinder shape. Kept on right leaving harbor; left returning.

Car A wooden slatted box, usually ten feet by fifteen feet by three feet, or larger. It is kept in the

Cage, Wheel and Rudder

water to store lobsters in until they are sold. Some lobstermen have their own cars and others are kept by the dealer. Lobster smacks come to some of the islands to pick up lobsters held there. A small car holds from 1500 to 2000 pounds of lobsters. See photograph.

Car with Shelves An older form of car which kept lobsters from bunching up and smothering themselves.

Carapace The forward shell of the lobster. See body.

Cashes (Ledge) One of the more common of the offshore fishing grounds, approximately eighty miles southeast of Portland, Maine.

Caulking Oakum and spun cotton which is used in the seams between the planks of wooden lobster boats to prevent leaking.

C.B. Citizen Band radios. These radios have been used for years by lobstermen who keep them in case of emergency. They can call other boats or shore stations within five to fifteen miles depending on weather conditions. Some lobstermen use them to talk to other fishermen while hauling. These radios are more frequently used than Marine Radio Telephones because they are cheaper and easier to get licenses for.

Chafing Gear Rags, rubber, or canvas tied around painter or hawser to prevent chafing or rubbing. Also refers to the slats on the side of the boat that prevent wear when hauling up traps.

Channel A clear path through the water among

ledges, islands, and shore that is deep enough for a boat to travel. In frequently used locations, channels are marked by buoys set by the Coast Guard.

Chart A navigational map showing the location of the shoreline, islands, reefs, ledges, wrecks, and navigational aids. Charts have the depths recorded in feet at mean low tide and also show the type of bottom. Usually used by experienced lobstermen only when they are out of their own territory.

Cheeserind Board inside the washboard around the hull. It is usually topped by an iron strip. Also called coaming.

Chicken Lobster A lobster size classification of between one and one-and-a-quarter pounds. Said by many to be the tenderest eating, though others say the large lobsters are no different.

Chock A fitting with two jaws curving inward, through which a line is run; used to prevent chafing.

Chop Small waves from local winds. Fishermen still fish in a fair (good-sized) chop if the fishing is good and there are no other bad conditions.

Chopping Tray A small boat, used in the manner of a skiff, for going back and forth to the mooring. It has straight sides and curved ends which make it resemble an old-fashioned kitchen chopping tray, hence the name. Also called punt.

Chum Cut-up fish used for the bait to toll (attract) mackerel.

Cleat A small piece of lath with curved ends which is attached to the door of the trap and around which is wound the end of the bait string. See photograph.

Clinch-Built Boat A boat built by nailing planks onto a frame and then pounding the nails over so that they are bent (or clinched) on the inside. This method of attaching the planks to the frame is cheaper than screwing the planks to the frame, but it is weaker.

Closed Season A certain time of the year when no lobstering is allowed. This has been advocated as a conservation measure for many years and is widely used in Canada. It has at this time met with only one successful reception in Maine, on Monhegan Island, where the lobstering season runs from January first to June twenty-sixth.

Coal Tar The substance that the pre-synthetic warps, heads, and bait bags were coated with to make them last longer. A big tar kettle was placed on the beach near the high water mark, and the tar was heated to the boiling point. Whatever was to be tarred was thrown into the boiling tar and almost immediately fished out with a pitch fork and thrown in the water. When the tide went out these items were picked up and taken back onto the bank. By that time the tar had cooled enough, so not much of it came off on the fisherman's hands. No longer used due to new materials.

Coaming Another term for cheeserind.

Cock Pit The entire open working area aft of the cabin bulkhead.

Cod End The end of the trawl net, which is a cone-shaped net. The fish are held here when the net is hauled up. This end has closer mesh and stronger twine.

Colors The particular buoy colors registered by each lobsterman that have to be displayed prominently on the boat. Fishermen try to choose colors that stand out in the water with one base color and stripes about the body and spindle of the buoy of another color. See buoy colors. See photograph.

Compass A device for telling direction. It consists of a card divided into 360 degrees with a fixed point at magnetic north. A compass course is run in the fog, rain, or snow, when a lobsterman can't steer by line of sight. He steers a known compass course from mark to mark. See photograph.

Co-op Cooperatives formed among lobstermen to eliminate the middleman in lobster marketing. Co-ops buy lobsters from their own members, charging a percentage for managing the co-op. They also sell fuel, bait, and other supplies at a lower cost to the members. At the end of the year the profits are divided among the members.

Coot A seabird often seen by lobstermen. Known for its "tough cooking."

Copper Nail A small nail used to fasten the heads to the frame of the trap. Copper is used because it doesn't corrode.

Copper Paint Paint used to paint the bottom of boats to prevent the growth of marine organisms. Dark red in color. Also called bottom paint.

Copy Cat A lobsterman who sets his traps where another fisherman does, particularly a highliner, in hopes of getting a bigger catch. Also called rudder fisherman.

Compass

Counter A lobster of legal size. A legally-sized lobster must have a carapace that measures between 3 3/16 and 5 inches in length.

Crab Trap A trap that is especially designed for crab fishing used mostly in the winter.

Cradle A heavily constructed device used to haul a boat out of the water for repairs, painting, etc. The cradle is put down the beach a-way and ballasted. At high tide the boat is floated onto it. After the tide goes out the cradle and boat are hauled up. See marine railway.

Crate A small wooden box, three feet by two feet by one foot, used for the temporary storage of lobsters. It is kept in the water on the mooring or behind the boat. Also used to ship lobsters short distances by truck. Some lobstermen put the lobsters directly into the crate on board the boat, but now most use a lobster box or tank. See photograph.

Crate Line Rope used for tying crates astern of the boat when at anchor.

Crib Work A kind of framework made of spruce or oak logs criss-crossed and filled with stone or granite as support for a wharf.

Cross Slats Structural member of the lobster trap running crosswise between the two sills.

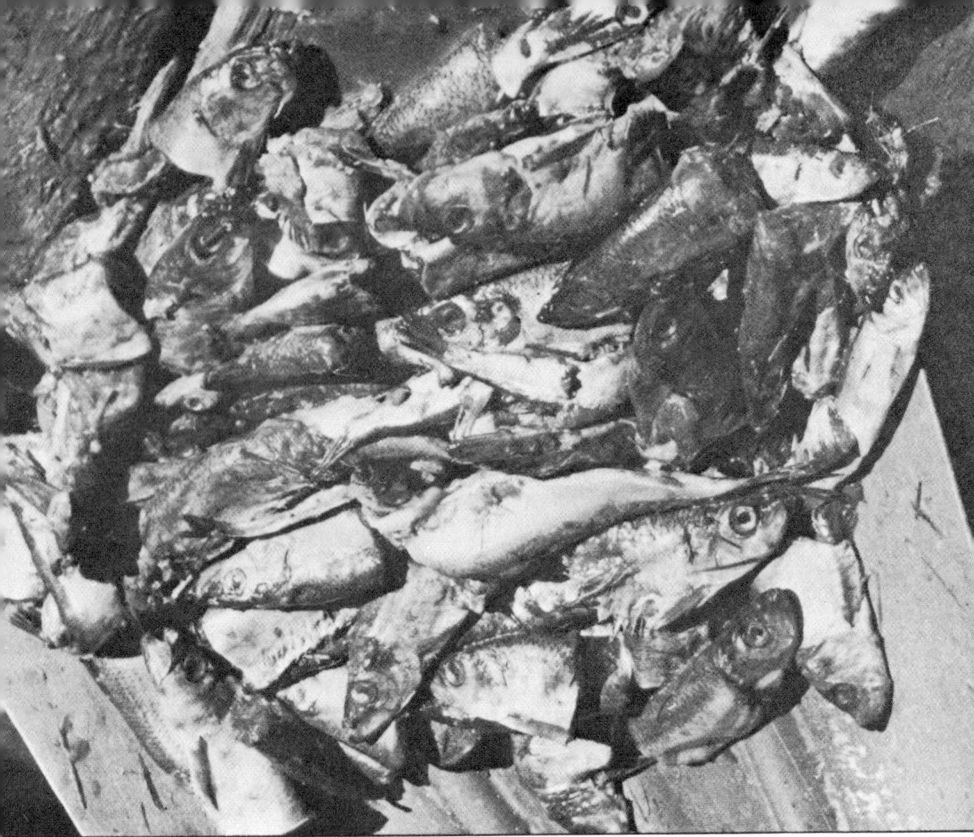

Cuttings

Crusher Claw The larger of the two lobster claws. Used by the lobster to crush its prey.

Cuddy Living area in the bow of the boat. Formally called cud. Used in the same manner as a forecastle on a large vessel.

Cull A lobster with only one claw. Usually sold at a lower price per pound.

Cunner *(Tautogolabrus adspersus).* Small fish formerly caught and used for bait in the old hoop net traps.

Cut Off The practice of cutting the buoys off the warps. Part of the tactics in a lobster war between lobstermen.

Cuttings Large herring cut into smaller pieces and used for bait; or the heads and tails of herring from the fish factory. See photograph.

Cut War Another term for lobster war.

D

Davit Arm (Davey Arm). Arm that supports the block for hauling. See photograph.

Depth Finder An electronic device which works on the principle of sonar by sending sound waves to the bottom and receiving an echo. The depth is shown by a needle or a flashing light on the dial. Some depth finders are equipped with a recording device which prints a continuous depth reading on a roll of paper. It is used when running, so the boat won't hit bottom. Also used when setting traps in order to find the edges of the shoal ground. Also called a fathometer or depth recorder. See photograph.

Devil's Claw Iron fastening device between the painter and mooring pole.

D.I.P. A homemade truck. As the fishermen gradually got out of the habit of having their own wharf and bait house and workshop, they took their traps to their home to work on them. That made a means of transportation for the gear necessary. Often that transportation was a D.I.P. or Deer Isle Pickup (localism). A D.I.P. was made from an older sedan with the body cut off just behind the driver's seat and a homemade truck-type bed added.

D.M.R. Department of Marine Resources. Formerly known as Sea and Shore Fisheries. This department does research for the industry and also regulates the lobstermen by means of wardens.

Dock A wooden, granite, or steel construction in coves and harbors which extends out into the water and provides a place to tie up for loading and unloading.

Dogfish *(Squalus acanthasis).* A spiny dogfish, which is a small shark that summers in great numbers in the Gulf of Maine. It frequently is caught in traps. It is considered a great pest. In England they are highly prized for fish and chips, but various attempts to market them in the United States have failed.

Dolphin Three pilings fastened together.

"Don't-She-Scale" Term that indicates a boat going at great speed. Originated with the fast schooners. The old-timers would say, "Don't she scale," making a comparison to scaling or skipping

FATHOM RANGE
0
FOOT RANGE
10
20
30
40
50
60
70
80
90
100
110
30
60
90
120
150
180
210
240
270
300
330
apelco
MS-602
DEPTH SOUNDER
OFF FATHOMS FEET
SENSITIVITY

rocks in the water. Means to have little resistance.

Door The top part of the lobster trap which is on hinges, opened to take out the lobsters, and to put in new bait. Constructed of laths and door cleats (frame) and attached by straps of leather or rubber. See photograph of door cleats.

Doors A large, very heavy rectangular construction of wood and iron which holds the trawl nets open under water.

Dory

Dory A common workboat along the coast, much used in the trawling and herring fishery. It has a sharp bow, flaring wide sides, a very narrow v-shaped stern, and a flat bottom. See photograph.

Double-Ender A boat with a pointed stern like the

Door Cleat

bow. These boats range from about sixteen feet to fifty feet. There have been a few lobster boats built as double-enders.

Doubles Fishing two traps on a single warp to save material and time in hauling. Also called pairs.

Doubling-Up Adding trailers to a single trap.

Dragger A general term used for any fishing vessel which tows a net. It may include a beam, trawl, otter-trawl, hake-mouth trawl, open trawl, scallop drags, or shrimp nets.

Dry Smack A boat which transports lobsters to the pound or market. It does not have holes to admit sea water like a wet smack.

E

Eel Grass *(Zostera marina).* A sea grass that grew on both sides of the Altantic and disappeared from both sides at the same time, during the 1930's. Used to be very thick in most of the coves and harbors of the Maine coast. It protected many of the small fish and provided an important part of the food chain.

Elastic Band of rubber used to keep the claws of lobsters closed so they won't cannibalize each other

Better than plugs which sometimes cause plug rot. Also called band.

End Buoy Last buoy in a lobsterman's string of buoys that are attached to traps. The end buoy is sometimes marked with a band or string on the spindle.

F

Fastenings Trunnels, screws, nails, bolts or any other device used to hold the planking and keel to the boat's frame.

Fathom A nautical unit of measure, six feet in length; usually refers to depth.

Fathometer Another term for depth finder.

Fetch-Up Refers to a trap catching on a rock or other impediment while being hauled. The fisherman will back off and pull from another direction to avoid damaging the trap or the warp.

Fiberglass Boat Lobster boat made with a molded figerglass hull which is usually finished with wood. Fishermen think the fiberglass hull is better because it requires far less maintenance and doesn't foul. Some fishermen still insist that a wooden boat is better, cheaper, and longer lasting.

Fillet The meaty section which is cut out of the sides of the fish.

Finest Kind The ultimate comment on quality—of the weather, the price, and even in one case, describing a drywall company on Bailey's Island. May go out of use from overuse.

Firing Phosphorescence in the water caused by dinoflagellates (small marine organisms). On calm nights when they are active any motion in the water stirs them and causes a brilliant shining. The brightness makes looking for herring easier.

Fisherman's Knot A knot used for tying warps together.

Fishing Inside Setting one's lobster traps close inshore, where the fishing is better due to the bottom, but where there is also more danger of running aground.

Fishing-in-the-Rocks Fishing close to the shore or the ledges during shedder season.

Fishing Outside Fishing outside the line of islands on the coast near the ledges and hard bottom.

Fishing Rights The privilege of lobstering in a certain territory. Fishing rights are obtained by inheritance, by being born in a lobstering port, family relationships, working as an employee or helper for someone who has rights; and occasionally by pur-

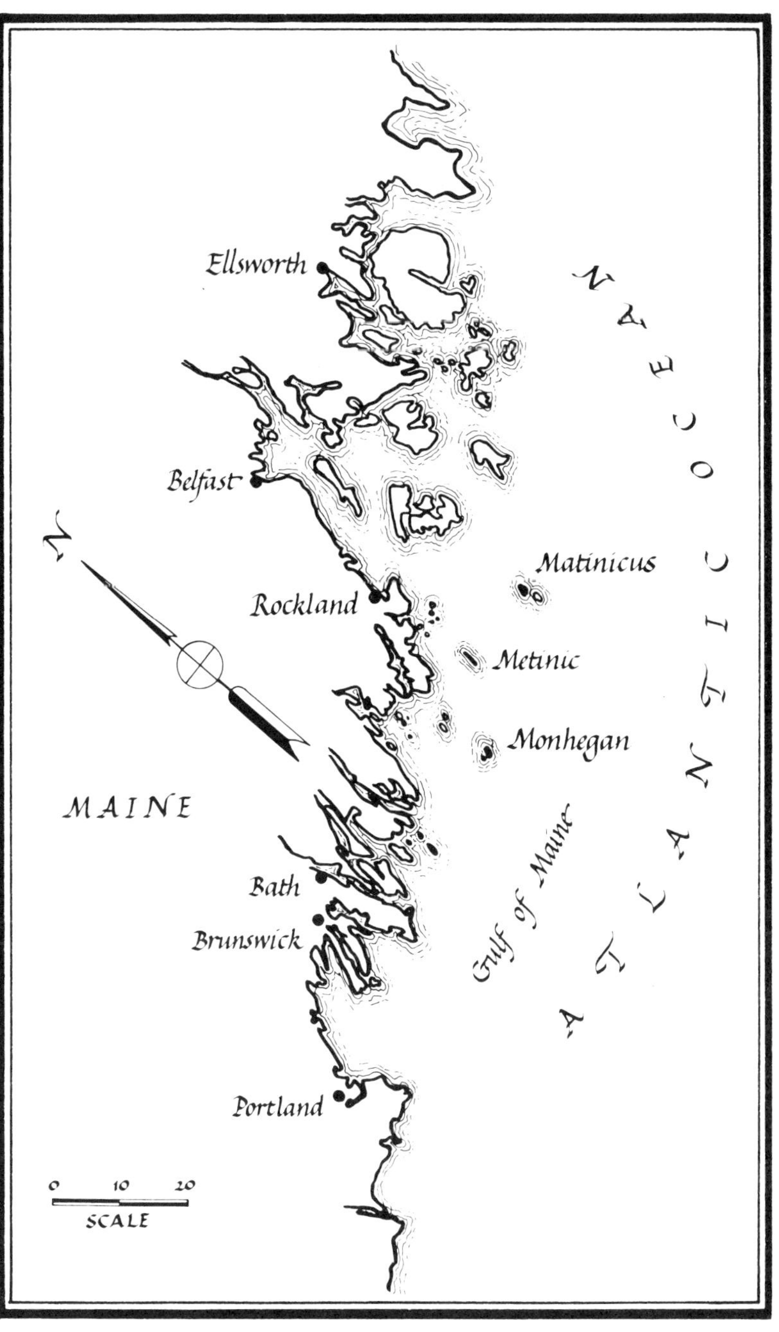
Ellsworth
Belfast
Rockland
Matinicus
Metinic
Monhegan
MAINE
Bath
Brunswick
Portland
Gulf of Maine
ATLANTIC OCEAN
N
0 10 20
SCALE

chase, particularly the rights around an island. Someone who doesn't have one of these "ins" is unwelcome and not allowed to fish. This has nothing to do with licensing—an unwritten law, in the manner of a tradition.

Fishing Trawls Fishing up to ten traps on one warp. This saves material and hauling time, but is a practice blamed by many for the overfishing in Casco Bay. Some areas have banned them. Also called gang.

Fishing in the Grass Ground Fishing close inshore where there used to be eel grass.

Flasher Flashing light on a depth finder.

Flat Ass Calm A condition existing when there is no wind, sea, or swell. This usually happens in the summer and frequently during a fog. Often pronounced "flat ars calm."

Flywheel Pin A pin that is put into the flywheel and used in starting the engine (one cylinder, two cycle).

Fog Horn A large horn driven by compressed air at lighthouses. Each has its own particular signal tone and rhythm, so that the fisherman can tell where he is without seeing the lighthouse. Also refers to a small horn carried by lobstermen run by lung power, now largely replaced by small horns run by compressed air.

Four Bow Trap A longer than usual trap with four

Four Header or Double Parlor Trap

bows instead of the traditional three; sometimes has a double parlor as well.

Four Header Traps with four heads; two side heads and two parlor heads, one behind the other. This arrangement is more efficient than the regular lobster trap in keeping the lobsters from escaping. See photograph.

Friendship Sloop A small gaff-rigged sloop, de signed by the McLeans of Bremem, Long Island, Maine, and the Morse brothers of Friendship, Maine, in the 1880's.

Fry Very small lobsters or fish which have recently hatched from eggs. Their mortality rate is extremely high.

Funnel Hoop Another term for funny eye.

Funny Eye A ring of metal to which the head of the lobster trap is attached and which keeps the mouth of the head open so the lobsters can enter the trap. Formerly made of bent spruce twigs, now it is made of copper or aluminum. Also called funnel hoop.

G

Gaff A tool for grabbing lobster buoys when hauling. It is constructed of a long wooden handle with a heavy wire hook at the end. The gaff is also used to grasp mooring lines, other boats, or the dock, when needed. It serves as a general extension of the fisherman's arm. In the earliest days of the industry it was used to fish for lobsters from small boats close to shore. See photograph.

Gang Fishing more than two traps per warp. Also called fishing trawls.

Gangion A line, smaller than the main rope of the trawl, that goes from the trawl to the hook.

Gaff

Garboard The first plank of the boat just above the keel.

Gear Another term for traps.

George's (Bank) One of the most fertile of the many fishing banks in the Gulf of Maine. It is located directly northeast of Nantucket.

Gill Net A net made of a certain size mesh which is suspended vertically in the water by means of floats and weights. The fish are caught by swimming into the net. As they try to back out, they catch themselves by their gills in the nets and can be hauled up.

Grassground Refers to area in the water that is close to shore.

Grassed Up Refers to buoys, warps, and traps when they are covered with slime.

Groundfish Fish that feed chiefly on the bottom of the sea, such as cod, hake, and sole of various kinds. They are caught by dragging a trawl along the bottom. Used as a classification in market statistics.

Guard A heavy strip of wood that runs the entire length of the hull of the boat, located at the top edge on the outside.

Gunnel The upper edge of the side of a boat. A derivative of gunwale.

Gurry Fish guts, scales, and other parts that get on fisherman's clothing and hands when baiting up and in other work about the boat.

Guy Lines Wires which help support the mast. Also called stays.

H

Hair-Toucher Term that refers to a measure. In the early part of the century, when they stopped measuring the whole length of the lobster, the State of Maine brought out a measure that measured from the end of the jibboon. On the back edge of the lobster body shell is a short row of hair, usually not more than one-eighth of an inch long. If the measure touched the hair on the lobster, the lobster was called a hair-toucher. Even though illegal a great many hair-touchers sold on the Boston market where the measure was smaller.

Hake Heads Fish heads that are used by some fishermen along with other bait when they are available from the hake fishermen. They are said to improve catches as they retain an odor longer than other bait, and do not tend to fall apart.

Hake Mouth Head A head on the lobster trap which is knitted to have a narrow opening into the

Hake Mouth Head

parlor which makes it more difficult for the lobster to get out. It is named hake mouth head because it resembles the mouth of the hake. Also called a skate mouth head. See photograph.

Halibut *(Hippoglossus hippoglossus).* A very large flat, white fish with very high quality flesh. It brings a good price. A number of lobstermen set out trawls for halibut in the spring.

Hand Line A fishing line made of heavy cord used to catch cod or other fish. Light lines are used for catching mackerel and pollock.

Harbor Porpoise A marine mammal, often seen by the lobstermen. Commonly referred to as a "puffer" because of the sound it makes exhaling air.

Hard Bait Pollock or whole trash fish used as lobster bait—not as good as herring or brim.

Hard-Shell Lobster A lobster whose shell has fully hardened after shedding. In the summer, hard shells bring a better price because they are meatier and have a better texture and taste.

Hatch Cover leading to an enclosed place on the boat.

Haul A term used to describe the work of the lobsterman. He says, "I'm going out to haul," not "I'm going out to lobster." Also used to describe the size of the catch. The catch might be described as "a good haul" or "the hauling is pretty poor on the west side."

Hauling Block A pulley located on the davit arm. It leads the warp to the pot hauler. See photograph.

Hawser A heavy line used for towing another vessel.

Head A funnel-shaped net that is attached to the openings in the trap and also is found between the parlor and the kitchen. The head allows the lobsters to enter the trap. Heads are usually knitted by the lobsterman himself. Formerly made of tarred marline

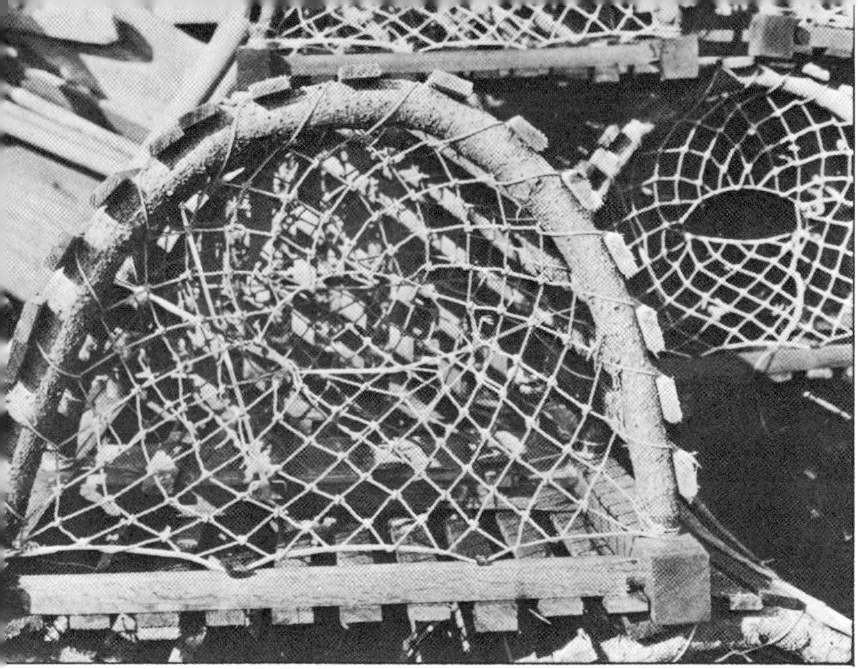

Head; Bough Bow

twine, now made of synthetic twine. Heads are also sometimes made of laths. See photograph.

Herring (Clupea harengus). Sea herring. A small, silver-scaled fish which lives in great schools in the Gulf of Maine. It is used as lobster bait and also canned as sardines. When used as bait it is salted down. See photograph.

Highliner A fisherman or lobsterman who has consistently the highest catches in his area due to skill and, some say, luck. Sometimes followed closely by copy cats.

Hinge A strap of leather, rubber, or metal used to hold the door onto the trap. Also may be made of pieces of rope or wire. See photograph.

Hinge

Hogshead A large barrel used to store bait. No longer used.

Hog-Yoke Trap A type of frame for a trap wherein the heavy framepieces goes across the bottom of the trap instead of along the side, as in a sill trap. The bows are attached to the hog-yoke; usually three to a trap, and cheaper than a sill trap to build. It gets its name from a similar yoke put on pigs to prevent them from getting out of their pens.

Hook Any of various sized heavy iron hooks used on board the boat to help in pulling and hauling. A large stainless steel hook is used for pulling halibut into the boat.

Hoop Net One of the earlier devices used to catch lobsters. This is a shallow net on a hoop or tire iron. Bait was placed in the middle of the net and it was lowered to the bottom for fifteen minutes or so, then hauled up. Whatever lobsters remained on the net were removed. This could only be done in shallow water at a time when lobsters were much more plentiful.

Hung Up Another term for fetched up.

Hydraulic Steerer Power-assisted steering now used by many fishermen.

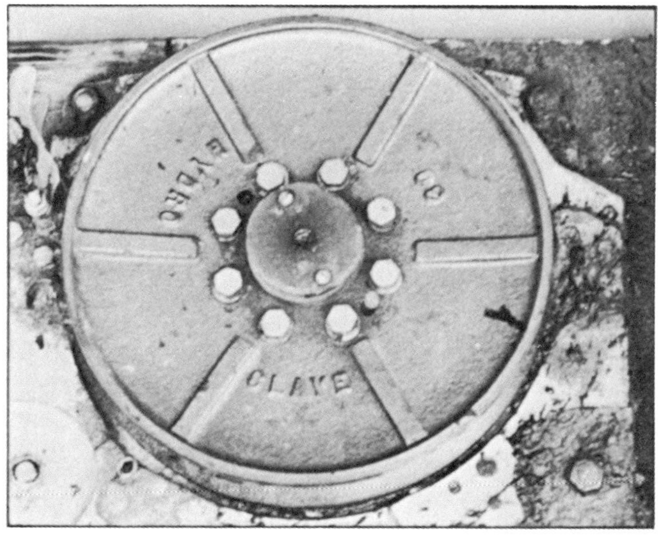

Hydraulic Drum

Hydraulic Trap-Hauler The most common means of hauling today. The lobsterman brings the warp over the block (pulley) which is hanging from the davit, and around the trap-hauler drum or sheaves. It is then turned on and the hauler hauls in the trap. See photograph.

Hydro-Slave A common brand of hydraulic trap-hauler.

I

Ignitor A device formerly used that was bolted to the top front of an engine on the boat to furnish the spark needed to start the engine.

In-the-Corner An expression that means the throttle of the boat is wide open.

J

Jonesporter A design of lobster boat which is low, narrow, and very fast. It is sometimes run by high powered car engines such as a Cadillac engine. It has been said that the design evolved from the rum-running boats of the 1920's.

K

Kelp A large undersea plant. It sometimes becomes entangled with the lobsterman's gear and causes difficulty hauling.

Hydraulic Hauler, Davit Arm and Block

Kitchen The first chamber in the lobster trap. The lobster enters the kitchen through the heads.

Knee Rail Another term for rail.

Knitting Needle A type of needle made of wood or plastic. It is flat, pointed on the forward end; and has two points on the back end with a partially hollowed center with another point. It is used to knit and repair nets, trap heads, and bait bags. See photograph.

L

Lead Line A measuring line to tell depths. It is marked by knots or colors into fathoms. The end is a lead sinker weight, which sometimes has wax in the bottom of it to pick up a sample of the bottom. It is said that some local navigators can tell exactly where they are in a fog by the type of bottom and the depth.

Lemonade Stand A term used to describe the glass and wood house on a lobster boat. Also called an Ash Point Piazza, or house.

License Each lobsterman or woman in the State of Maine has to have a license. There are about 7,000 licensed lobstermen in Maine, but many of these are not full time. Some fishermen think that licenses will become limited and increasingly difficult to get, so have bought them for their wives and children.

Knitting Needles

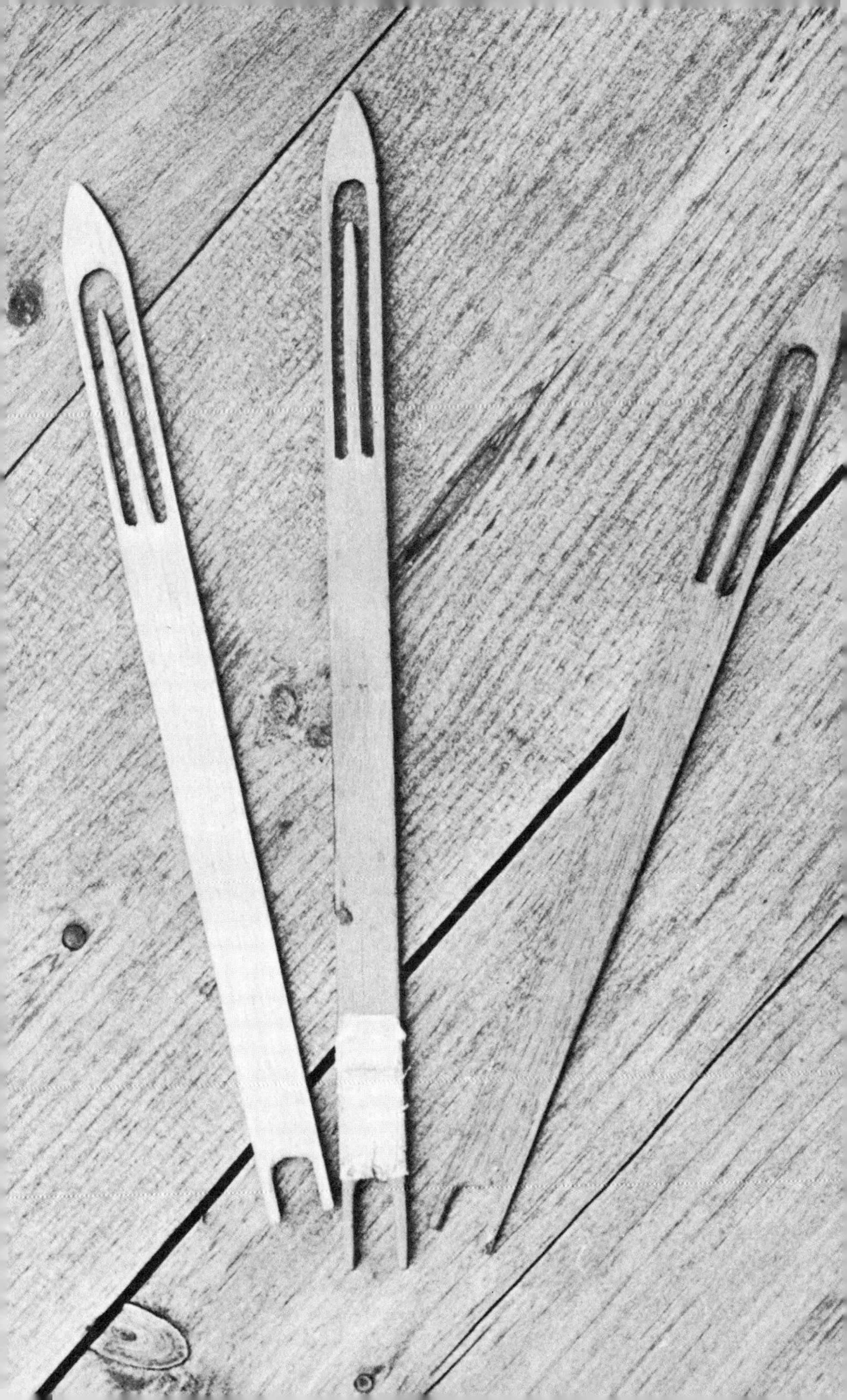

Line The nautical term for rope of most sizes. Also refers to the place where a lobsterman's specified territory for fishing ends and someone else's begins. Also refers to the equator.

Line Storm A heavy storm that occurs in mid-September when the sun crosses the equator or "line." Frequently does extensive damage to traps.

Lobster (Homarus americanus). The true American lobster, a large edible marine crustacean which is caught in traps by fishermen. Considered the pinnacle of a fine dining experience whether served plain boiled, baked stuffed, in lobster stew, lobster salad, lobster sauté, lobster newburg, or lobster thermidor. See photograph.

Lobster Boat Races Races held each fourth of July near Jonesport, Maine, to determine the fastest lobster boats in Maine.

Lobster Bottom A good ocean floor for catching lobster. It is usually rocky as this type bottom provides caves for the lobsters to hide in.

Lobster Dealer Dealers or middlemen in every lobstering port who buy lobsters from the lobstermen and also supply them with bait, gas, and supplies. Some dealers are employed by companies and some are independent. Now being challenged by Co ops.

Lobster Factory Plants where lobsters were cooked and canned in the 19th century for shipment all over

Lobster, Homarus americanus

the world. Some say this led to the first great depletion since they used small lobsters which had not yet bred. Eventually, size limits eliminated the factories.

Lobster Festival The Maine Seafood's Festival held the first weekend of August each year since 1948. It is part carnival, part fishing history, part craft show, and is all the celebration of Neptune and his gifts. This festival is held in Rockland, Maine—the lobster Capital of the world.

Lobster Fisherman's Style A special, old-fashioned way of cooking lobster with canned milk. See cooking section.

Lobster Metinic Style See cooking section.

Lobster Stew A rich hearty stew of milk, cream, and lobster. See cooking section.

Lobster Tank A sea water filled container on board some lobster boats which holds the lobsters and keeps them alive. Also refers to the large bins inside lobster pounds where lobsters are kept awaiting shipment to market. Refers, too, to the tanks in markets and restaurants throughout the country that keep lobsters alive for consumption.

Lobster War An argument over territorial fishing rights which can manifest itself by the cutting of buoys (and resulting loss of traps), and more occasionally with the ramming of boats or even gunshots. This is the Maine equivalent of a range war. A recent lobster war on the Maine and New Hampshire border had to be settle by the United States Supreme Court.

Long Day-Short Day The staggering of hauling traps so that one day more traps are hauled and the next day fewer are hauled.

Long Warp A trap set deeply enough so that it requires twenty to fifty fathoms (120 to 300 feet) or more, according to the fishing grounds. A lobsterman refers to these traps as long warps rather than deep traps. Shallow traps, or traps set in shallow water, are known as short warps.

Loran Long range aid to navigation. Used by the offshore fishermen. This device helps them determine their precise position or longitude and latitude. Called loran lines.

M

Manila A kind of rope made from hemp. Not now as widely used as rope made of nylon or other synthetics.

Marine Railway A set of old railroad tracks placed on ties on a beach on which the cradle sets. The boat is placed on the cradle and hauled out on the marine railway to be worked on. The cradle is usually hauled up by a winch attached to a block and tackle. Sometimes greased planks or beach rocks instead of tracks are used for pulling up the cradle. See photograph.

Marks Anything that a fisherman gets his position from, such as a buoy, a church steeple, or a ledge. Frequently when traveling on the water the fisherman will go from mark to mark.

Marline A thin cord formerly used in making heads and bait bags. Largely replaced by synthetics.

Mast A short upright spar on the stern or just behind the house on the lobster boat. Some lobster boats have a small sail on the mast to keep the boat headed into the wind when hauling at a slow speed. Some masts are used as derricks.

Measure A brass measuring device used to measure the length of a lobster. It hooks into the eye socket of a lobster and down the length of the body or carapace. If the length is from 3 3/16 to 5 inches the lobster is of legal size and can be sold, all others must be thrown back. See photograph.

Mesh Board A small piece of wood or plastic used in combination with the knitting needle to knit heads and bait bags. See photograph.

Monel An alloy of stainless steel used in shafting and also in fastening the planks to the hull.

Marine Railway, Cradle

Mooring A permanent anchor in the port where the lobster boat is based. It consists of a long wooden pole with a hole at one end for tying the boat. A chain is attached to the other end which is in turn attached to a mooring rock, which is usually a large piece of granite. Some lobstermen also have a mooring at their island fishing grounds. A chain mooring has a buoy instead of a pole.

Mosquito Fleet The boys and girls of the various lobstering ports who fish a limited number of traps in small boats during the summer. Sometimes the fleet is resented by adult lobstermen because the youngsters can fish closer in shore in their smaller boats. Graduates of the mosquito fleet often become fulltime lobster catchers.

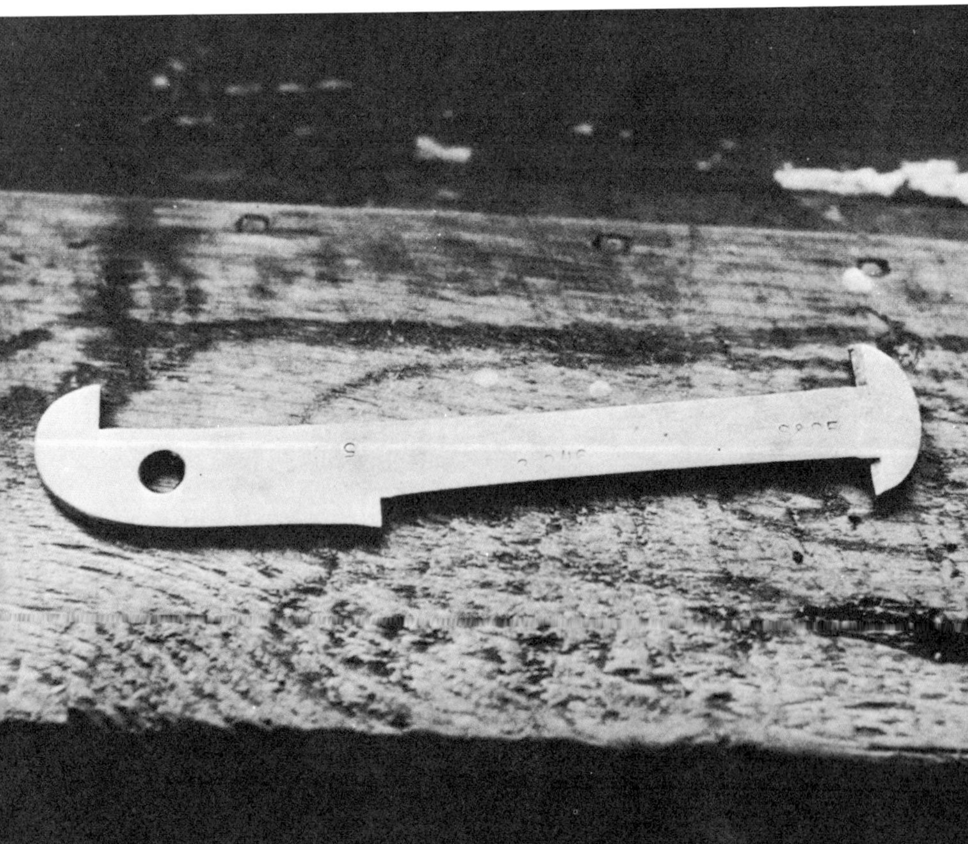

Mesh Boards

Moving Gear An expression that refers to looking for a better fishing bottom. Also called shifting gear.

*Niggerhead** A commonly used term for winch head.

**Publishers Note:* The term "Niggerhead" appears in this book because it is an established and authentic lobstering term. The wooden winch to which it referred is now extinct and the publisher is pleased that the name is passing with the outdated equipment. The term appears in this book for accuracy, not because the publisher condones its use.

Numbers

Nippers Gloves, that are quite similar to wristers, except they are not as wide and are knit thicker.

No'theaster A storm with the wind blowing from the northeast. Causes heavy seas and brings rain or snow. It can cause severe damage. Often referred to as a "no'theast gale."

Novie Boat A large lobster boat built in Nova Scotia for about half the price of an American-made boat. Wide, as well as long, they supposedly don't last as long, but are bought due to the low initial cost.

Numbers The registration number of the lobster boat which must be painted on both sides of the bow. Also refers to the fisherman's lobstering license number, which is branded on the buoys and on the traps (or written in the wet cement of the traps). See photograph.

Nun Buoy A tapered red metal buoy used as a navigational aid. Boats keep them to port outbound, starboard inbound. The phrase used to designate the nun buoy is Red Right Returning. The opposite buoy is called a can buoy and is a wide black cylinder.

O

Offshore Wind Wind blowing from the Northwest.

Oilskins The rubber coat, pants, and hat used by the fishermen in wet weather or when handling wet nets or trawls. This waterproof clothing used to be made of cloth treated with linseed oil, hence the term "oilskins."

One Claw A lobster that has lost one of its claws. It usually sells for less to the dealer, although the lobsterman is paid by total weight. Also called a cull.

One Lunger A one cylinder, two cycle engine used in the early days of motorized lobstering. Also called a make-and-break engine. Some of the more common of these engines were the Bridgeport, the Knox, the Casco, the Hartford, and the Essex.

One or Two Prices Refers to the different prices of soft-shell and hard-shell lobsters. There is one price until the shedder season starts.

Onshore Wind Wind blowing from the south or east, or southwest.

Otter Trawl Large cone-shaped net held open by doors. Used for catching groundfish.

P

Packing Gland Flax packing to insulate the propeller shaft as it goes through the hull.

Painter A line or rope used to tie up the boat. Also called a pennant.

Pairs Fishing two traps on a single warp. Also called doubles.

Parlor Trap The inner chamber of the lobster trap. The lobsters get to the parlor by going through the kitchen (where the bait is) and then through the large head. The head into the parlor is larger than the head which the lobsters entered through. Though some lobsters do eventually get out of the trap, most remain in the parlor. Also called a bedroom trap.

Parted Refers to a broken warp.

Pea Pod A small, sixteen foot or so, double-ended rowing boat. Its name derives from the shape. Used in early lobstering.

Picked Meat The meat of the lobster picked out of the shell for shipment or canning. It takes approximately five chicken lobsters to produce a pound of picked meat.

Pickle Another term for bait juice.

Piling A long wooden pole used as part of a wharf or dock. It is secured in the ground underwater and supports the wharf or dock.

Pincher Claw The smaller claw of the lobster used for tearing pieces off its prey and bringing them to its mouth.

Pistol A lobster which has lost both its claws.

Planing Refers to certain designs of lobster boats which rise up on the water and go faster on a level keel.

Plastic Boat A boat made of fiberglass.

Platform The floor inside the rail on the boat which serves as a work area.

Plug A small pointed piece of wood or plastic which is inserted into the outside of the thumb of the lobster claw. This prevents the lobsters from fighting in the pound. It sometimes causes a disease known as plug rot; also it can cause the lobster to "throw" his claw. Usually, only the crusher claw is plugged, but some fishermen plug both claws. Now replaced in some parts of the coast by banding.

Plug Box A container to keep lobster plugs in before plugging.

Plug Rot The disease which causes decay and blackening of the claw flesh around the plug.

Pogy A fish that sometimes shows up in great number on the coast of the Gulf of Maine. When available, it is used for bait. Also known as menhaden.

Pot Another name for trap; used interchangeably. The term pot derives from the conical French and English lobster and eel pots.

Pot Hauler Refers to either a hydraulic hauler or a winch head.

Pot Nails Three penny, fine galvanized nails that are used to nail the laths onto the frame of the lobster trap.

Pot Warp A small-sized, twisted, three-strand rope attached from the trap to the buoy. Used to haul up the trap. Once it was made of sisal or manila and tarred, but is now made more frequently of nylon or

polypropolene. The newer materials last longer than the older forms of warp. See photograph.

Pound A storage area for holding lobsters keeping them alive. It is usually made by closing off a small cove. A slatted gate allows the water to flow freely in and out. Lobsters are held in this manner in order to get better prices in off-seasons. There is substantial risk of loss due to disease or cannibalism and over-feeding. Some lobster companies keep lobsters in tanks in buildings with constantly circulating water. These are also called pounds.

Pound-Keeper A manager of a lobster pound, who often serves as the dealer as well. He may work for self, a company, or a co-op.

Poverty Boxes A name some lobstermen use for their traps.

Propeller Pitch The distance in inches that the boat propeller moves through the water with each revolution.

Puffer A common term used by lobstermen to refer to a harbor porpoise.

Punched Lobster A female lobster that has had a hole punched in its tail, to notify the other fishermen to throw it back overboard for breeding purposes. An alternative to V-notching. Also may cause disease.

Punt A type of small boat that some lobstermen use

as a tender. It has a flat bottom, which curves up at the ends and straight sides. It can be loaded with a large amount of goods or supplies. A skiff is referred to as a punt in some areas of the coast. Also called a chopping tray.

Purse Seine A method of catching herring. The school of herring is spotted by a plane or boat, the seiner moves to the area, encircles the fish with a net which is then closed or "pursed" at the bottom. The net is then drawn into the boat until the fish are brought together. They are pumped into an accompanying vessel called a sardine carrier. The carrier then takes the fish to a plant for processing for food or for use as bait.

R

Racks Fish bait. Head and bones of fish after it has been filleted.

Radar A radio direction finding device which shows boats the location of ledges and shoreline in fog, snow, rain, or at night. Only a few lobster boats have radar, although most larger vessels do.

Recorder Automatic electrical depth recorder. Also called fathometer.

Redfish *(Sebastes marinus).* A small groundfish

Ring, Staple

caught in great numbers in the Northwest Atlantic. The fish is filleted and marketed under the name of Ocean Perch. It is generally not eaten in Maine. The head, backbone, and tail that remain are used as lobster bait; probably the most common bait, since it is available year-round.

Red Tail A fast-moving disease, mostly in pounds, caused by bacteria. It is very contagious and apt to be caused by over-feeding.

Reduction Gear A gear mechanism that converts the high speed of the engine to the lower more efficient speed of the propeller.

Riding Sail Lobsterman's term for a staysail.

Ring-and-Staple A large staple which holds a metal ring onto a wooden buoy to which the pot warp is fastened. No longer used. See photograph.

Rock Crab A small crab that gets into the lobster trap to take the bait; somewhat of a nuisance, though a number of lobstermen save and sell them to processors who pick out the meat and sell it. It has a much finer texture and a sweeter taste than Alaskan crab.

Round Trap A half-round trap made by using semicircular bows for the top frame.

Rubber Stopper A plug used in glass toggles. See photograph.

Rudder Fisherman A fisherman who follows a highliner and sets his traps in the same place. Also called a copy cat.

Running Lights Red, green, and white lights on a lobster boat that show at night so that other boats may see them. White for stern, red for port, green for starboard.

Running Under Refers to the dragging of buoys underwater by a strong tide or current.

S

Sardine Carrier A medium-sized boat, fifty feet or so in length, that carries the catch of herring from a purse seiner to a sardine factory.

"Scale It Overboard" An expression that means, "Throw it overboard."

Scaling Fog A term that refers to the fog lifting.

Scallop Drag A small net with an iron blade attached to the bottom and front. It is hauled behind a dragger or lobster boat and scoops up the scallops on the bottom. This activity usually takes place in the winter and provides some off-season income for the lobstermen.

School A large group of fish of a single species which swim together for protection. Herring and mackerel school near the surface, and can be spotted and purse seined. Groundfish can be spotted near the bottom with a fishscope. Some older lobstermen claim to have seen thousands of full-sized lobsters schooling near the surface, although scientists claim this is impossible.

Scow A large rectangular wooden float used for hauling buildings, vehicles, and other large objects from the mainland to the islands.

Sculling A form of rowing using one oar from the stern of the rowboat.

Sculpin A nuisance fish often found in traps.

Scupper A hole in the side or the stern of the boat which allows the water which has accumulated on the platform to flow out.

Scupper Plugs Plugs used to close scuppers at the platform level.

Sea A big rolling wave created by a storm that is some distance away, or by a gale in the local area.

Sea Anchor A canvas pocket put over the side into the water to keep the boat headed into the wind. It may be used when working on the engine.

Sea and Shore An abbreviation for the Sea and Shore Fisheries Department that is still used, even though the name has been changed to Department of Marine Resources.

Sea Cock A valve that allows salt water to come into the boat through a hose for cooling the engine or washing down the deck.

Sea Fleas Tiny crustaceans which eat the bait in the traps, or anything else dead. They are often seen on beaches as well.

Sea Gull A bird in constant company with the fishermen. The bird is particularly looking for the old bait the fisherman throws over the side. The most common is the gray-backed herring gull, though now there are a considerable number of black-backed Arctic gulls. They nest on many of the islands that are good fishing grounds.

Sea Smoke Vapor over the water when the temperature drops below zero.

Sea Urchin (Strongylocentrotus drobachiensis). A sea animal with a round shell covered with dozens of green spines. It is attracted to the bait in the trap and is a nuisance to the fisherman. The sea urchin is eaten in some European countries and by people of European descent in America, so fishermen occasionally have a market for them. Also known as whore's eggs.

Seeder A pregnant female lobster carrying her eggs on the bottom of her tail. Seeders are supposed to be thrown back overboard as a conservation measure.

Seine Net used for catching herring. When it is used to close off a cove full of the fish it is called a stop seine. When used in open water and gathers fish at the bottom, it is called a purse seine.

Seiner A boat that catches herring and transfers them to a sardine carrier. See photograph.

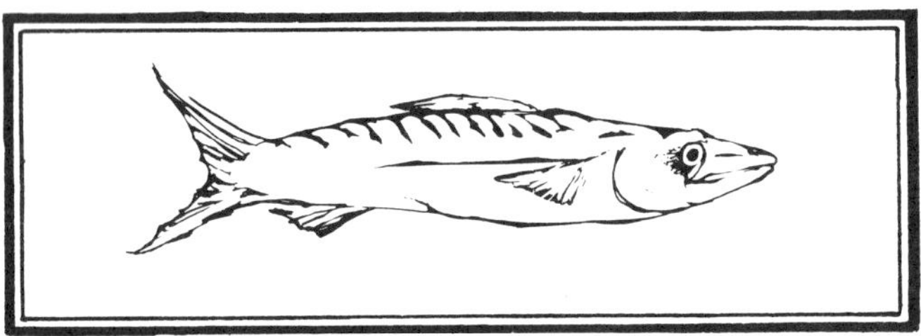

Self-Bailing Cockpit A boat on which the platform is higher than the waterline and the water on the platform automatically runs out the scuppers.

Set Term used to describe the placement of traps. Also called setting.

"Setting in the Woods" Derogatory term for a lobsterman who sets his traps close inshore.

Shag A cormorant. A black, fish-eating bird common around the lobstering grounds. Also called a shitpoke.

Shares The system of profit sharing used on two-man lobster boats and on most larger fishing vessels. Shares might be forty per cent of the profits from the catch for the boat, thirty per cent for the lobsterman, and thirty per cent for the sternman; or by the day plus a percentage rate of the catch. This varies with locality.

Sheathing A covering of thin sheets of copper below the water line on some wooden lobster boats. Sheathing prevents fouling of the wood by marine organisms and damage by marine borers.

Shedders Lobsters during their molting stage. This usually occurs in the late summer or early fall. The lobster sheds his whole shell in order to grow. Shedder (or soft-shelled lobsters) bring a lower price than hard-shelled lobsters because their meat is not as firm and is quite watery.

Sheer Refers to the line along the top of the hull sides, as viewed from the side.

Slack Ballast

Sheer Strake The top plank on the hull.

Shelldrake A common sea duck frequently seen by the fisherman. Also called merganser.

Ship to Shore Radio Usually refers to a marine radio telephone. The fisherman calls an operator in a central area and is hooked by telephone to the person he desires on shore.

Shitpoke A name commonly used by fishermen for both shags and herons because of their habit of dropping waste every time they take off.

Shoal Water Shallow water.

Short A lobster under the legal size. Said by some

Skiffs

to be very tender eating. Also called snapper.

Short Warp The designation used for traps fished in relatively shallow water. This is usually twenty fathoms or less as opposed to long warps for the deep fishing during fall and winter.

Shrinkage The death of lobsters in storage either on the mooring or in the pound.

Sill A piece of oak along the bottom sides of the trap which forms the frame. The bows are attached to the frame.

Sinker Rocks Slack ballast put in the wooden traps when they are first put overboard until the traps soak up.

Skate Mouth Head Another term for hake mouth head.

Skeg The keel onto which the hull of the lobster boat is built. It contrasts with built-down boat in which the keel is part of the hull.

Skiff A small boat used as a tender by lobstermen. Usually has a sharp bow and a square stern. It is usually rowed, but sometimes powered by a small outboard motor. See photograph.

Slack Ballast Rocks put in dry traps till the wood soaks up enough water to establish the proper buoyancy. See photograph.

Slack Water Refers to the time when there is no current, just before the tide turns. Also called slack tide.

Sleeves Knitted woolen sleeves that cover the lobsterman from his gloves to part way up the arm. Sleeves prevent chafing from the sleeves of the oilskin.

Smack A small boat which sails from lobster shipping ports to the islands to pick up lobsters from the cars they are stored in. These boats take the lobsters to port to be shipped to various destinations. Some of the smacks are wet carriers with holes in the storage compartment in the hull to allow salt water to flow in.

Smokey Sou'wester A southwest wind with a lot of haze in the summer. It makes it difficult for the lobsterman to see long distances.

Snappers Shorts. Lobsters of an illegal, too small size.

Snatch Block The block or pulley that is used to guide the warp onto the hydraulic pot hauler.

Soft-Shell Lobster A shedder. Remains a soft-shell until its shell hardens up.

Sounding Machine Another name for a depth finder.

Sou'wester Hat worn with oilskins. It has a large

back brim to prevent water from going down the back of the neck.

Spar Buoy Long pole anchored by a chain, painted black. This used to mark channels before the advent of the nun and can buoys.

Spindle A wooden rod that forms the handle of the lobster buoy. It sticks out of the conical top end of the buoy and helps make it show up in the water. Also refers to a tall iron rod with a barrel or marker on top that marks the location of a ledge.

Splice A method of interweaving two pieces of rope to make a smooth join. See photograph.

Sprayhood A canvas screen on the bow of the boat to protect the fishermen and boat from spray and wind. It can be easily taken off. Sprayhoods have largely been replaced by houses.

Spray Rails Strips fastened lengthwise on the hull, slightly above the waterline, to help minimize the amount of spray coming aboard.

Squall A strong wind which comes up quickly, often with rain or snow. It can be dangerous, but usually does not last long.

Square Trap A rectangular flat-topped trap, used by some fishermen. It is easier to build than a round trap and also easier to stack. It, however, is not as strong as a round trap.

Splices

Stays Another term for guylines.

Staysail A small sail on the mast of the lobster boat used to keep the bow of the boat into the wind while hauling at slow speed. Also called a riding sail.

Stem Iron A metal strip fastened to the outside of the point on the bow (stem) to minimize abrasion.

Sternman A man who empties the traps, rebaits them, and puts them overboard. Paid in shares or per diem. Only used by fishermen who have a great number of traps that could not be hauled profitably alone.

Sticking Tommy A metal device with two points

Square Wire Trap

which was stuck into the side of the hold of the fishing vessels. A candle was stuck on the other point giving light for loading. No longer used.

Stop Seine See Seine.

String A particular line of traps in a certain area, usually of the same warp length. Also, all of the traps one lobsterman fishes, "He has a string of 350 traps."

Stuffing Box Refers to all of the packing and bearings that prevent water from entering the hull where the propeller shaft passes through.

Styrofoam Buoy Buoys made of styrofoam. These have largely replaced the wooden (usually cedar)

buoys of the past. They have a high flotation ability and do not get as waterlogged as the wooden buoys. However, they present a problem in that sea gulls eat them. See photograph.

Swell A wave made by winds that are out to sea. The wave is smooth and rolling, and has no crest or sharp chop.

T

Taking-Up-Gear Putting gear on the bank. This is done at the end of the lobstering season, or to dry the traps out.

Territory The area which a specific lobsterman can fish as determined by unwritten, but traditional usage. If a fisherman is lobstering in someone else's territory he is usually warned by a knot around his buoy spindles. If he does not take heed and stop fishing the territory, the buoys are cut off.

Thick-A-Fog A manner of saying there is a heavy fog.

Thick-A-Snow A manner of saying there is heavy snow.

Thick-A-Vapor Description of the vapor that forms over salt water when the temperature is below zero.

Styrofoam Toggles

Thole Pins The wooden rods attached to the gunnels of a dory to hold the oars in place while rowing. Used in place of oar locks.

Toggle A flotation device tied part way down the warp to keep it off the bottom and prevent it from fouling. Toggles used to be empty liquor or soda bottles with rubber stoppers. These glass toggles have been replaced by doughnut-shaped pieces of styrofoam which are less fragile and less dangerous. See photographs of glass toggle and styrofoam toggle.

Tomalley The liver of the lobster. Essential to good lobster stew.

Torching A method of attracting herring by burning a torch at night in a cove..Used frequently in the past to get bait—it is now illegal.

Torpedo Stern The torpedo stern boat was popular for awhile at Swan's Island, Maine. It was a double-ender, but the stern curved in toward the boat as it went up. This took a lot of room that could have been used to store traps on the stern. Use of the torpedo stern boat for lobstering did not last long.

Tour-Ast Season A lobsterman's pronunciation of a summer phenomenon that occurs annually in Maine.

Trailer Second trap in a double.

Trap The cage-like structure used for catching lobsters. Until recently, it has been usually constructed of a wooden frame which is enclosed by oak laths (strips). Bait attracts the lobsters to the trap and they crawl through net heads to get into the trap. Traps are lowered into the water, their location marked by buoys, and are checked periodically by hauling to the water surface. Newer traps are now being made of wire or plastic. Also called lobster pot (after European usage). See photograph.

Trap Day Monhegan Island has the only limited season on the coast of Maine. Today this is called conservation, it used to be called common sense. The season begins on the first of January and lasts until June twenty-sixth. The lobstermen all set their traps

Glass Toggle

Traps

on the same day unless one of the fishermen is sick or injured. If this occurs they wait, until they all can start to haul on the same day.

Trap Mill A saw mill that cuts the oak frames and laths for traps.

Trap Smasher A bad storm, such as a line storm, or a hurricane, that destroys many traps.

Trap Stock The wooden parts of the trap that come from the trap mill; laths, sills, and bows.

Trawler A large diesel-powered fishing vessel which tows the trawl net.

Trap Frame, Bows, Sills

Twine A thin cord used in the knitting of bait bags, trap heads, and other nets. Formerly made of cotton line and tarred, but now replaced by longer-lasting nylon cord.

Two-Header A lobster trap with two parlor heads. Also called a four-header.

U

Up Forward Refers to the enclosed part of the boat in the bow in front of the house. Serves as a shelter and sometimes as an engine room. Some have bunks and a stove. Also called a cuddy.

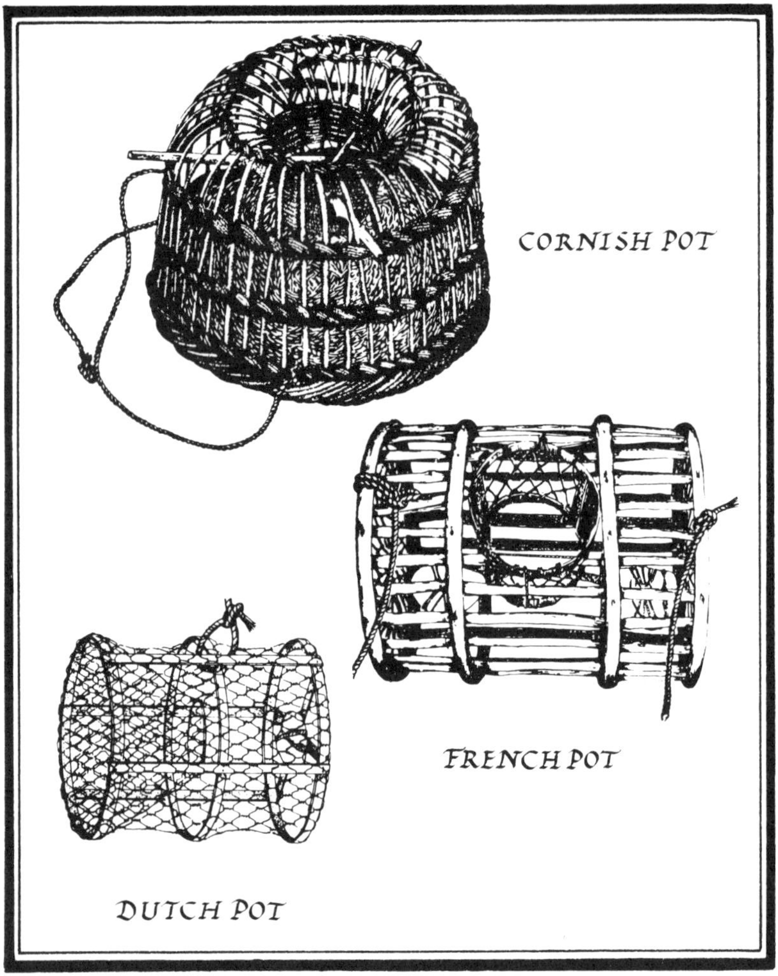

CORNISH POT

FRENCH POT

DUTCH POT

V.H.F. Very High Frequency radio used by some fishermen; replacing older type ship-to-shore A.M. marine radio telephones.

Double Header
cover
laths
button
bow
exterior view
entrance
bait bag
entrance
runner
ballast
interior view
hinge
entrance
runner
end view – both ends
Parlor Trap
entrance
exterior view
parlor
entrance to parlor
entrance
bait bag
ballast
interior view
cover
hinge
button
end view – both ends
Buoys
main buoy
bottle toggle buoy
pot warp
trap
bridle

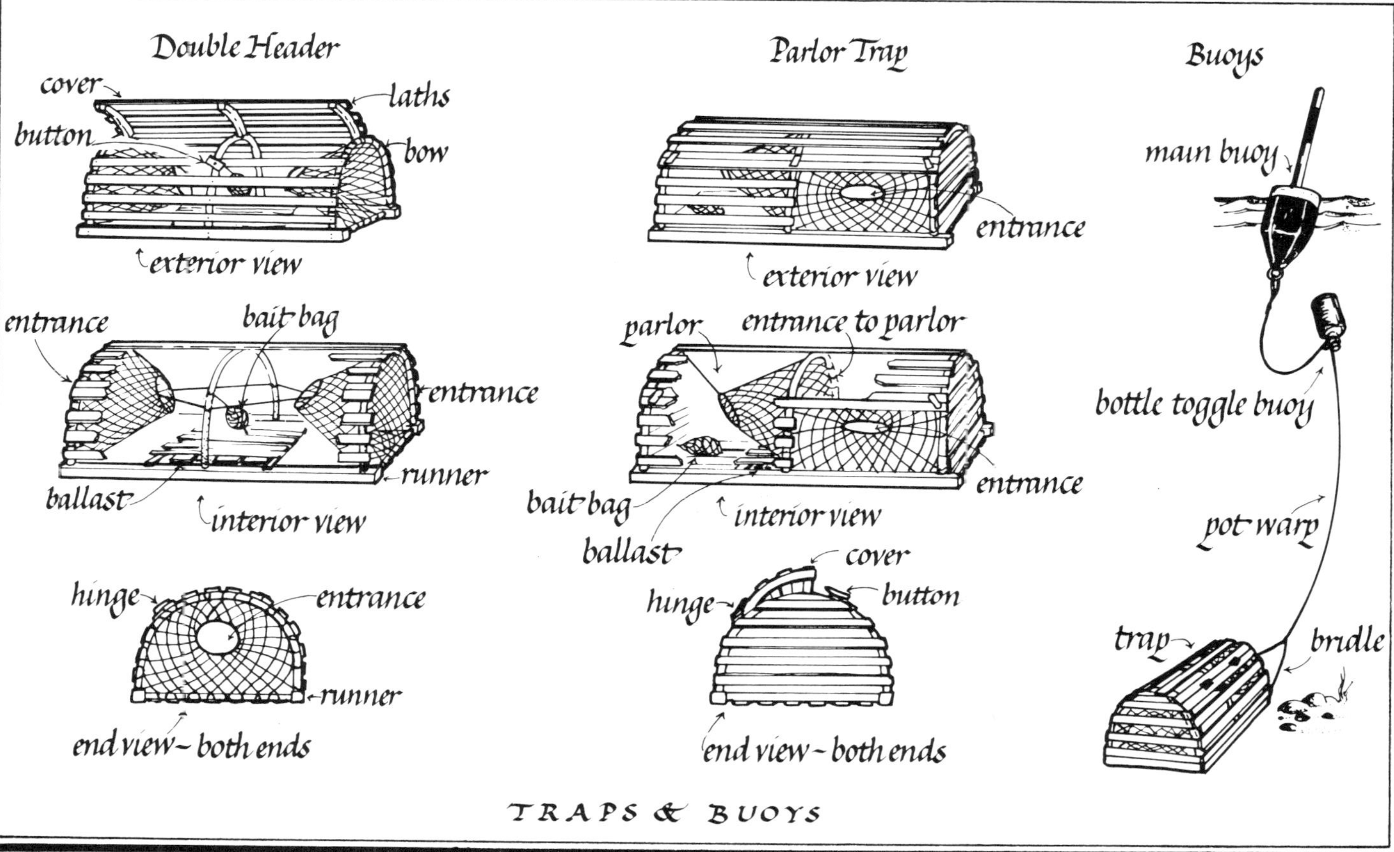

TRAPS & BUOYS

V-Notched Lobster The practice of cutting a V-notch in the tail of female lobsters before throwing them back, so other fishermen would not keep them. The practice is being discontinued because the cutting can cause infection.

Warden The policeman of the Department of Marine Resources. The department has the power to bring fishermen to court for fishing violations such as possession of short lobsters or fishing someone else's traps.

Warp Common term for pot warp.

Washboard Decking between the coaming and the outside of the hull.

Weir A trap for herring or salmon made of a fine mesh net. In the past there were many of these along the coast which helped to supply bait and sardines; largely replaced now by purse seining.

Wet Smack A smack used for going long distances. They have a compartment that is separated from the other parts of the boat, which has holes to the outside of the boat so that fresh saltwater can flow through and keep the lobsters alive. Also called well smack.

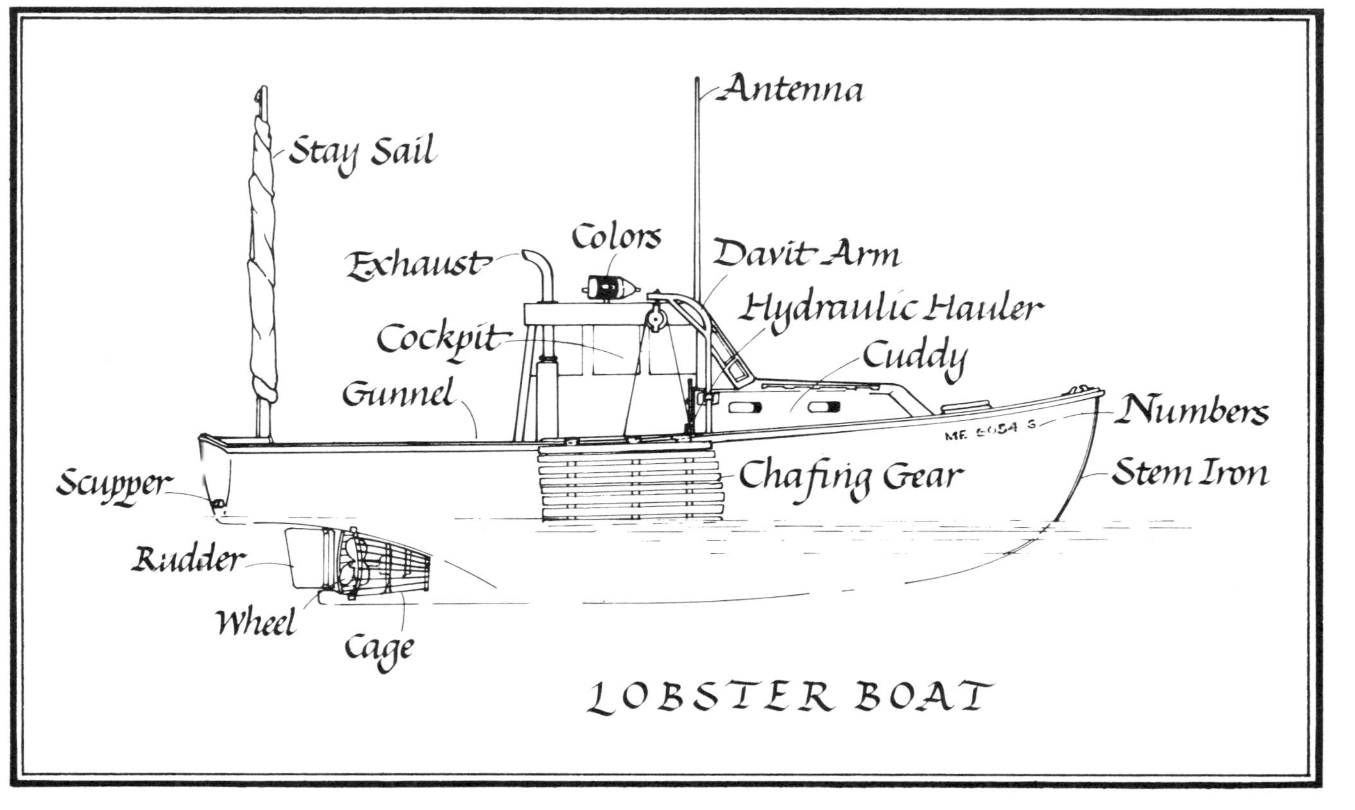

LOBSTER BOAT

Winch Head

Wharf A dock made of wood or stone which extends into the water from the shore. Provides space for boats to tie up and load or unload.

Wheel Propellers are referred to as wheels by the fishermen.

Whistle Buoy Automatic buoy placed by the Coast Guard that has a whistling sound which warns boatmen of a hazard.

Whore's Eggs Another term for sea urchins.

Wire Trap A square trap made of plastic-coated or aluminized wire. One fisherman claims they last as long as the wooden ones, (2½ to 3 years) and that they fish just as good. Several firms in Maine

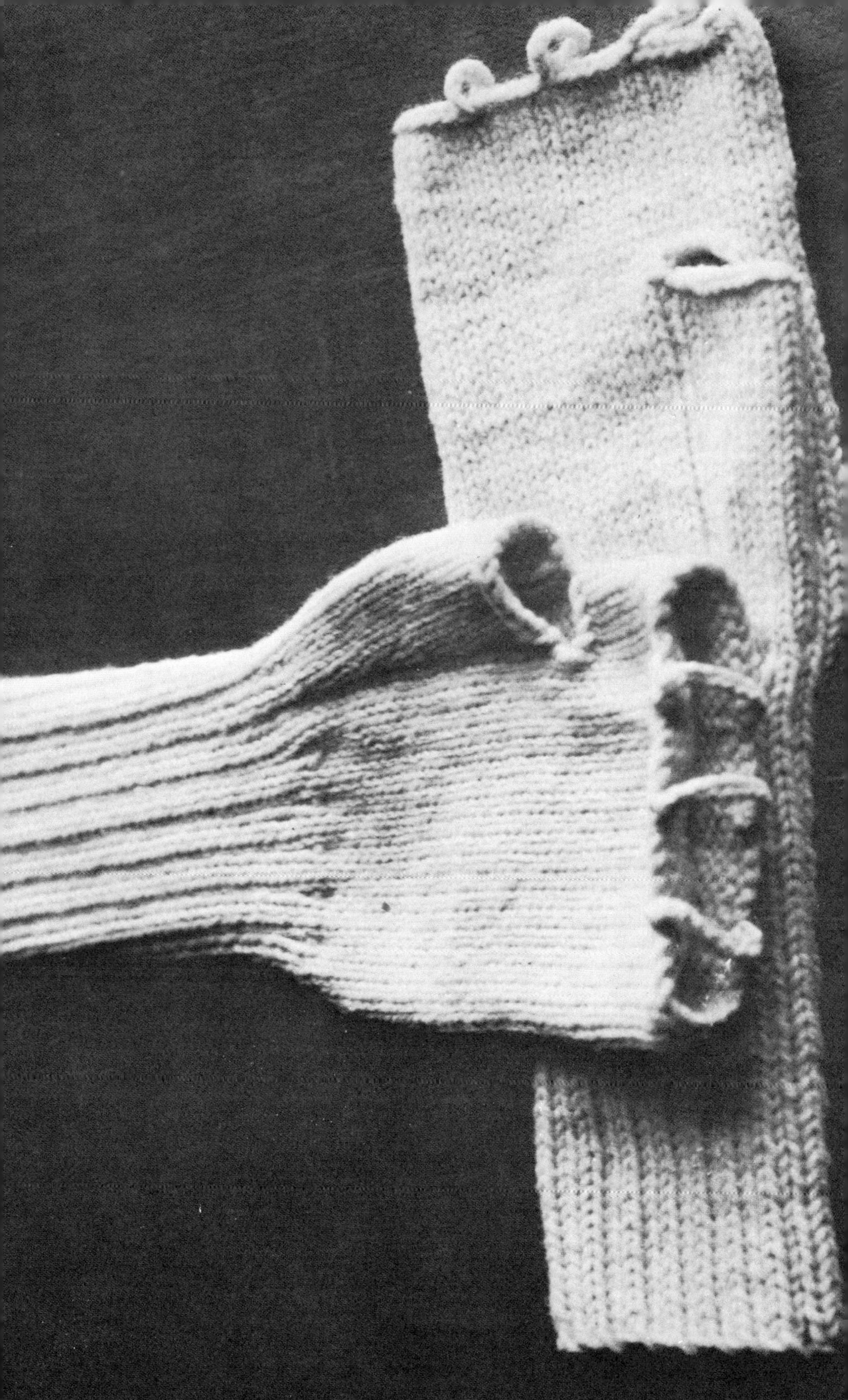

manufacture them and some lobstermen make their own. They are light in weight; they do not need slack ballast; and are easier than wooden traps to store, stack, and handle. See photograph.

Winch Head A bronze bell-shaped cylinder which revolves from power geared from the engine. The pot warp is thrown around the head and it hauls the pot up. Largely replaced by hydraulic pot haulers. Early ones were made of oak. See photograph.

Wristers Knitted woolen gloves, with no fingers, which prevent chafing caused by the oilskins; and which allow freedom of movement for hauling. Also protects from the cold. See photograph.

Recipes

The Maine Way of Cooking Lobsters

I present here four ways of cooking and serving lobster that I can certify are Maine methods: one came from a lobstering family, one from the son of a lobster dealer, and two are my own.

There are many fancy ways of cooking lobster, but most of the lobster dishes I have been served are elegant in their simplicity, with lots of fresh lobster. Contrary to many out-of-staters opinions, most Maineacs do not eat lobster every week. It is a treat for them, and even lobstering families are conscious of saving next year's haul. We usually have them in the summer when the price is low, and we like more than one apiece, depending on how we are cooking them.

Lobsters should be obtained live and kept alive until cooked. They should not be stored in fresh water or on ice. They usually can be successfully kept alive overnight in the least-cold part of the refrigerator, such as in the vegetable bin or some other cool place.

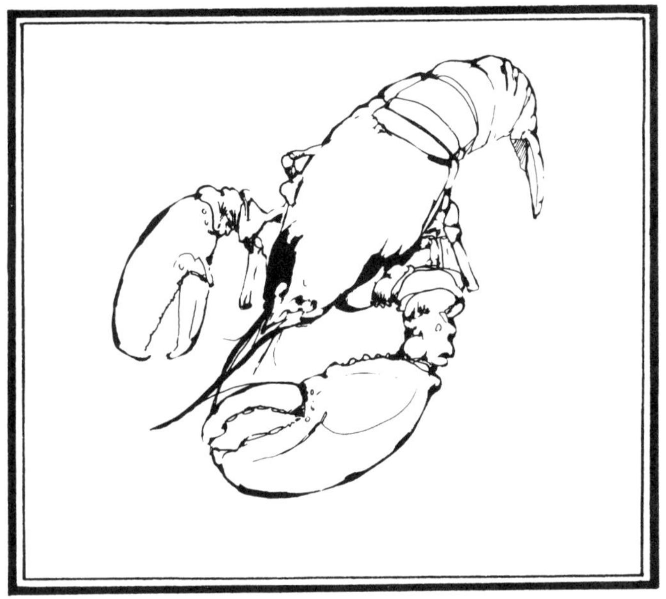

Basic Boiled or Steamed Lobster

Fresh clean sea water; or fresh water, with salt added
One or more live lobsters per person
Melted butter
Lemon wedges

The most traditional way of cooking lobsters is to boil them. For this you need a large pot with a cover. Fill the pot two-thirds full of fresh clean sea water; or fresh water, well salted. Bring to a boil, put in whole live lobsters, and cover pot. Bring the water to a second boil. Set timer for desired time. Cooking time varies along the coast. Stephen Cook boils lobsters for fifteen minutes, or until they turn bright orange-red; my Father cooks them for eighteen minutes; and on Metinic lobsters are cooked for twenty minutes. Twenty minutes is the most usual time.

I prefer to steam my lobsters rather than boil them. I place just a little water (or, heaven forbid, beer) in the bottom of the pot. I cook them, covered, eighteen minutes after the second boiling. This method is faster and keeps the lobsters more firm.

After the lobsters have been removed from the pot (for which tongs are very useful), let them cool until you can touch them. Serve immediately with melted butter and lemon wedges. Remove the meat from the shell, dip in melted butter, squeeze lemon over the meat, and eat with fork or fingers.

Lobster Fisherman's Style

Bill Butman, a Spruce Head lobsterman, was helping me at an exhibit at the Lobster Festival in 1973, when he told me about this well-loved family recipe for lobster which reflects the traditional use of canned evaporated milk along the coast.

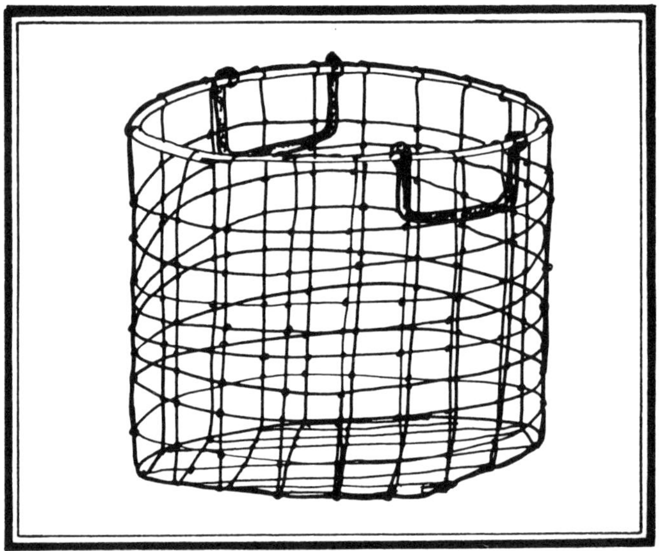

Lobster, one per person
Butter
Canned evaporated milk

Boil one lobster per person. Let cool to touch. Pick out the meat and cut it into good-sized pieces. Leave the knuckles whole. Sauté in plenty of butter for three to five minutes over medium heat (too hot and too long makes it tough). Pour canned milk over the lobster, enough to cover the bottom of the pan, plus a little more—half the depth of the lobster. Remove from heat, let set a couple of minutes, covered. Serve immediately on a dinner plate with mashed potatoes and peas.

Baked Stuffed Lobster Stephen Cook

Stephen Cook is a young poet who is the son of the owner of Cook's Lobster Pound and Restaurant on Bailey's Island, Maine. He has worked in the pound and the restaurant for a number of years. He developed for his personal use, baked stuffed lobster, which is different from the usual dish, both in its richness and its piquancy.

"Lobster may be cooked in steaming water; or on the shore, steamed with clams, corn, and Maine potatoes. But I like to bake-stuff my lobster for the richest flavor. Baked in the oven is one way of cooking the lobster within the shell so it cooks in the juices

of its own claws and body. My stuffing includes saltine crackers, green peppers, onion, garlic, pepper, and lobster."

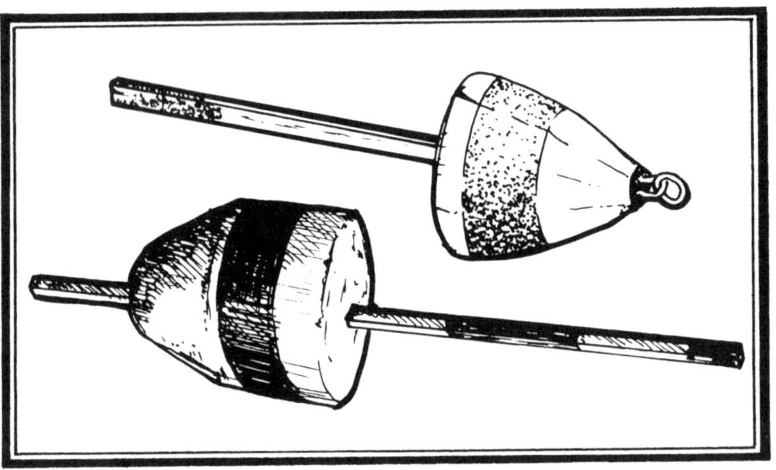

Fistful of saltine crackers, crushed
2 tablespoons green pepper, chopped fine
2 tablespoons onion, chopped fine
Garlic, one clove, or to taste, chopped fine
Pinch of pepper
Meat of a one-pound boiled lobster
Cheddar cheese (optional)
One-pound live lobster

Mix all of the ingredients together, except cheese and live lobster. Be sure to include the juices from the boiled lobster body. If you need more moisture in the stuffing, melted butter may be added, or lemon squeezed into the mixture for a slightly tangy flavor.

Hold the live lobster by the claws firmly and with a

large knife cut an opening in the stomach from the head to the tail. Remove heart and intestines. Lightly press the stuffing mixture into the spread opening until full. If the lobster is a soft shell, you may want to wrap the claws in tin foil to keep them from burning.

The stuffed lobster should be cooked twenty minutes in a 375° oven. About five minutes before the lobster is done, you may sprinkle cheddar cheese over the stuffing to melt.

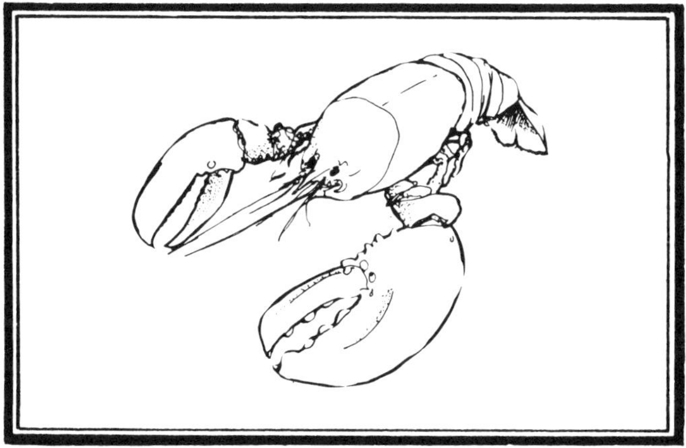

Lobster Stew

I developed this recipe after a period of experimentation. It is actually quite simple and probably similar to the stew of many Maine cooks. A *sophisticated* guest from Philadelphia once told me it was one of the finest dishes he had ever eaten.

8 live lobsters
4 tablespoons butter, or more
1 pint heavy cream
reserved liquid from lobsters
a half gallon of milk, or more
salt and pepper to taste

Steam or boil the lobsters eighteen minutes, place cooked lobsters on several platters to cool and catch juices. After cooked, pick meat from lobsters taking care to get the green liver (tomalley) out of the body cavity. Reserve the tomalley, and any coral found. After the meat is all picked out, sauté tomalley and 1½ tablespoons of butter in a heavy cooking pot.

After three or four minutes put more butter and some of the lobster meat into the pot. Repeat this until all the lobster meat has been sautéed for five to ten minutes. Add the cream, the reserved juice, and the milk. Simmer on low heat, taking care not to boil or cover, for several hours. Salt and pepper to taste.

If you have the patience, make a day ahead. It improves the taste. I have never had the proper resistance to do this.

Serve with a good white wine, oyster crackers, salad, wheat or yeast rolls, and a good dessert. This is as close to royalty as you can get in Maine.

Kendall Merriam was born and grew up in Rockland, Maine, which is known as the "Lobster Capital of the World." He attended Gordon College in Wenham, Massachusetts, where he studied history and government; graduating in 1965, with a B. A. In 1968, he attended the Munson Institute of American Maritime History at Mystic Seaport. In 1969–70 he worked as assistant curator at the Bath Marine Museum. He has published articles of maritime interest in *The National Fisherman, Downeast, Maine Issue, Maine Sunday Telegram* and in the book *Gulf of Maine*.

Ed Wheaton, the photographer for the book, grew up on Swan's Island, off Mt. Desert Island. He lobstered while growing up and his father is presently a lobsterman. He spent three years in the U.S. Army as a photo lab technician. He has since worked for the Army Topographic Commission, freelanced for Stevens Studio in Bangor, Maine, and is currently a photographer for the Maine State Archives.

If the reader has any comments, clarifications, or suggestions for additional terms the author would appreciate the information.

Please write Kendall Merriam in care of the publisher.

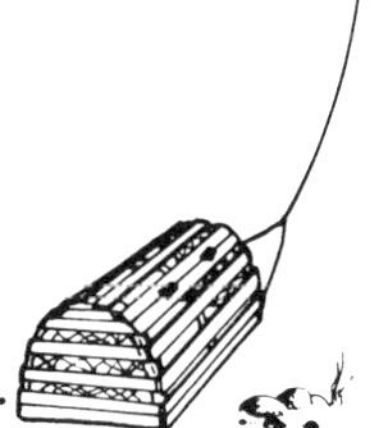